Bitcoin

I0484090

The Ultimate Guide for Understanding Bitcoins And What You Need to Know

Table Of Contents

Introduction

This short book is for people who are interested in learning more about the Bitcoin currency and are not sure where to start or what information to rely on. The Internet has a ton of articles and misinformation about Bitcoin that confuse people who are interested in learning about this revolutionary crypto-currency and possibly interested in purchasing some bitcoins themselves.

In this book I am going to give you a short, concise guide for everything you need to know to get started with Bitcoin. Understanding the history of this currency as well as the current innovations that are going on in the Bitcoin market are key to predicting what the future will hold. We will also go over the different functions and options that a person has when it comes to purchasing their own bitcoins and how to use them.

Most importantly, we will go through the pros and cons of using Bitcoin so that you can understand everything you need to know before taking the plunge and investing in it yourself. Whether you plan on diversifying from fiat currency, starting your first crypto-currency with Bitcoin, or you just want to know more about why this trend is becoming so popular, it is important to objectively see all the benefits and risks involved.

As a side note, I recommend that you take notes while you are reading this book. This will ensure that you get the most out of the information in here. I want you to feel that you made a purchase that is worth your money and so that you can look over the notes of this book even after you've finished reading it. The notes will help you to pinpoint exactly what you need to implement, and by writing things down, you will be able to recall specifics and how to handle certain situations when they arise.

Lastly, remember that everything in this book has been compiled through research, my own experiences, as well as the experiences of others, so feel free to question what you have read in this book. I encourage you to do your own research on the things that you want to look deeper into. The more you understand about

Bitcoin, the more educated your decision-making process will be when it comes to purchasing and transacting your own or when giving advice to others.

Chapter 1:

What Is Bitcoin?

Bitcoin as an electronic currency, is transacted around the world through the internet. Today, more businesses than ever accept Bitcoin as payment for goods and services. It can be considered as a mode of payment just like credit cards or PayPal. It is a repository of money which can be spent, traded, and/or transferred from one location to another without paying hefty fees.

Bitcoin allows transactions to occur anonymously. This means that when a person receives some bitcoins, it is possible that he/she doesn't know the real identity of the person who sent the digital currency to him/her. As such,

Bitcoin may be used for illegal transactions. However, even if the real sender is a mystery, transactions are done in public view through the internet and can be publicly monitored.

Although faced with legal issues, Bitcoin is actually an innovative digital currency which can break barriers between different nations, as well as free the currency from manipulation and control of governments. It is operated using mathematics and controlled by software and individuals who ensure the currency is running as expected. The open-source software is collectively operated by different individuals around the world.

Important Characteristics Of Bitcoin

No Central Control

Bitcoin can not be manipulated and/or controlled by just one authority. Its network is composed of different computers scattered around the world and monitored by ordinary individuals. As such, no central authority can decide on monetary policy. No government can seize bitcoins or artificially inflate the value of them.

Ease Of Set Up

Individuals have to go through a lot of procedures to be able to open a bank account with a traditional bank. Merchants also have to submit many documents if they want to accept another mode of payment. Bitcoin doesn't require any of this. Anyone can use a Bitcoin wallet, set up in just a matter of seconds. The acquisition and maintenance of owning a Bitcoin wallet is even free of charge.

Anonymity

A Bitcoin address isn't linked to a public personal identification. A person can have multiple Bitcoin addresses without formally linking them to his/her true identity. This anonymity is very attractive to people who feel like their normal day-to-day transactions are being monitored way too much in the fiat system we are currently operating in.

Transparency

Every Bitcoin transaction is kept in an online ledger which is available to the public for scrutiny. Anyone can find out how many bitcoins are stored in a particular Bitcoin address. However, no one knows who owns that particular Bitcoin address except its owner (and whoever they tell).

Low Or No Transaction Fees

Bitcoin doesn't charge fees for transfers or transactions. This is a huge advantage over systems like PayPal or most other online money-holding accounts.

Fast

Bitcoins can be sent anywhere in the world in just a matter of minutes. The recipient can receive the bitcoins once the network verifies the transaction. In most cases, it just takes around 10 minutes for the process to be verified by a Bitcoin miner - much less than the standard 2-5 business days by banks.

Non-refutable

Bitcoins can not be returned unless the recipient agrees to send them back to the sender. This prevents charge-backs and many cases of fraud.

Chapter 2:

How Bitcoin Came To Be

Satoshi Nakamoto, a pseudonym, is regarded as the creator of Bitcoin. No one really knows the identity, or identities, of the people behind the pseudonym. Bitcoin is designed to be maintained by various computers around the world connected through the internet. Anyone can join this network if he/she knows how.

The Bitcoin mining software creates bitcoins, which are just digital balances and addresses kept in a digital ledger known as a blockchain. The system is designed wherein Bitcoin creation is timed. Individuals who maintain the computers are responsible for the growth of the digital currency. They monitor the transactions and update the ledger. In return, they are rewarded with a certain amount of bitcoins. Currently, about 25 bitcoins are created every 10 minutes.

Bitcoin production is limited to a 21 million cap. It is estimated that the upper limit will be reached by around 2140. Because the digital currency is created by machines, no government controls it. If the maximum number of bitcoins has been reached, it is expected that the Bitcoin's value will rise because more people and businesses will create a demand.

Although the creation of new bitcoins are projected to stop around the year 2140, the electronic currency can still be easily spent because it is broken down into 100 million units, where each unit is called a Satoshi.

Chapter 3:

How The Bitcoin System Works

The basic principle behind Bitcoin is cryptography. This means that everyone who has even a fraction of a Bitcoin is an owner of a private key that gives them access to an Internet address where the Bitcoin balance resides in the online Bitcoin ledger. It is the possession of that key and the Internet address which provides proof of Bitcoin ownership.

The Internet address can be distributed to anyone who uses Bitcoin because it is where payments are sent. A person or business entity can not send bitcoins to the intended receiver without that address. Basically, the Bitcoin sender needs his/her own Bitcoin address as well as a private key so that they can send Bitcoins to the receiver.

The key is required to authorize the transfer of bitcoins. When bitcoins are sent to a receiver, the transaction must be checked by a Bitcoin miner before the transfer is approved. Because math is part of the whole Bitcoin system, the transaction must be checked mathematically. A transaction can be rejected if the Bitcoin miner can't verify the math.

A Bitcoin wallet is a digital wallet which monitors the Bitcoin transactions of sending, receiving, and transferring. Private keys and Internet addresses may be difficult to manage, especially for people who aren't adept with technology. The wallet may be installed on a personal computer or mobile device and can even be kept on a website. By owning a Bitcoin wallet, it will make transactions easier.

However, Bitcoin transactions can also occur offline. A mobile Bitcoin wallet makes it possible for a person to pay a brick-and-mortar business establishment with bitcoins. A QR code of the business can be scanned using a mobile phone.

Chapter 4:

Reasons For Using Bitcoin

Faster Transaction Processing

In a traditional setup, it takes a few days for a bank to clear a check - same with international wire transfers. The long processing time is needed to ensure that the payer really has available funds. Bitcoin transactions, however, take only about 10 minutes to be verified. The receiver can even opt for zero confirmation if he/she wants an instantaneous transaction.

Cheap or No Transaction Fee

Unlike credit card or debit card transactions, the Bitcoin network doesn't charge transaction fees. If ever it will charge for processing, it will be very minimal as compared to traditional card transaction fees.

No Central Authority

Bitcoin is decentralized. As such, no single government can seize it even when it wants to. This is a huge draw among libertarians and those people who have issues with fiat currency and the Federal Reserve.

No Chargebacks

A Bitcoin can't be returned to the sender unless the receiver sends it back. This means an unscrupulous person can not make chargebacks, which can easily occur in credit card transactions.

No Personal Information Theft

Credit card information is often stolen when a card is used online. Most online merchants require the buyer to furnish the information onto their website. Thus, hackers and lawless elements can easily steal the information, especially if the site isn't very well secured.

Luckily, Bitcoin users have the assurance that this won't happen to them. They can give away their public keys or Bitcoin addresses but hackers still can not get into their accounts unless these criminals know their private key as well. Unless users give away their private key, no important information can be stolen.

Not Affected By Inflation

Fiat currency has an inflationary nature because the central bank can print unlimited bills. If there is a lot of money in the market, then the currency will naturally decrease in value. In essence, inflation causes the price increase of goods and services. It can also cause the decrease of buying power for the citizenry. Bitcoin is not subject to inflation because production is limited to 21 million only. In fact, deflation may occur when the maximum number of bitcoins has been reached.

No Trust Issue

In traditional banking, a person needs to trust other people that their money is handled properly. They need to trust the payment processor as well as the seller. These people can ask for sensitive yet important personal information from the person. On the other hand, there is no need for trust in Bitcoin transactions. No one really needs to know the person behind the transaction, as long as the funds are sent.

Ownership

Traditional electronic cash systems are often owned by third parties. As such, the third party can decide to freeze any account if the account holder doesn't follow its rules. On the other hand, a Bitcoin account is owned by the account holder. He/she owns both the public and private keys related to a Bitcoin address.

Opportunity To Mine Bitcoins

Unlike fiat money, which is printed by the central bank, bitcoins can be produced by anybody who has the resources and time to do so.

Chapter 5:

How To Obtain Bitcoin

Get A Bitcoin Wallet

To get bitcoins, a person must first have a Bitcoin wallet, which can be downloaded from bitcoin.org or other related websites. A Bitcoin wallet is like a physical wallet which can store money. In the case of bitcoins, it is an electronic wallet where the electronic currency may be stored.

It is possible to keep the wallet on a person's hard drive or they can avail to online Bitcoin wallets being offered by some websites. If the wallet is stored on a personal computer, it is important to have backup so that the bitcoins aren't lost if the computer crashes. On the other hand, an online wallet may be subject to hacking and other attacks, especially if the website isn't secure.

Bitcoin Exchanges

In the United States of America, a lot of people troop to the Coinbase website to transact bitcoins. Coinbase charges a 1% fee to act as the proxy. It links the individual's bank account and acts as an exchange for Bitcoin transactions. It also has its own Bitcoin wallet. Bitstamp or Mt. Gox are large exchanges where bitcoins are also traded. However, these websites require cash payments through wire transfers, which can be slow and expensive.

For individuals who are interested in speculation and trading, having an account with a Bitcoin exchange can be beneficial. A person who wants to avail this service may be required to provide documents to ascertain his/her identity because governments now require this from exchanges to prevent money laundering and other illegal activities.

Over The Counter Or Meetups

Bitcoins can also be purchased through meet ups. A person can search for another individual within the community who sells his/her bitcoins. LocalBitcoins is a website where people can find other people selling bitcoins through meet ups. Individuals who sell bitcoins often require cash transactions because bank and credit card transactions are reversible. Because meetups have security risks, it is important for both the seller and the buyer to meet in a public place. A laptop, tablet, or smartphone with internet access is required.

There are also people who organize large bitcoin meetups. A person may even meet new friends in the process. Some sellers add, at most, 10% to the current Bitcoin price to cover the costs incurred in meetups.

Bitcoin Mining

Additionally, a person can also get bitcoins by mining. To become a miner, a person needs a computer that is connected to the Bitcoin network through peer-to-peer technology. The computer also needs the Bitcoin software. Currently, Bitcoin mining has become difficult and only professional miners can afford the expensive processing power of a custom-designed computer.

Investment Trust

The Bitcoin Investment Trust is offered to those individuals who don't want to store Bitcoins with them. It is the trust that ensures bitcoins are kept safe for its shareholders.

Bitcoin ATMs

A relatively new concept, there are some Bitcoin ATMs currently in existence. At this time, a person can buy bitcoins through the Bitcoin ATMs. He/she inserts cash in the slot and a transaction receipt is printed after the successful transaction. The receipt contains codes that the buyer will need in order to load the bitcoins to an electronic wallet.

Chapter 6:

How To Store Bitcoin

As previously mentioned, bitcoins are stored electronically in what is known as a wallet. A private key is needed to access this Bitcoin repository. A Bitcoin wallet can take many forms, depending on the kind of device - it can even be a paper storage. It is important to keep the wallet secure and have a back up in case the wallet becomes corrupted. In essence, it's the private key that is stored in the wallet and not the   bitcoins.

Desktop Wallet

A Bitcoin wallet can be installed on a person's personal computer. Bitcoin.org has Bitcoin-Qt, a software which installs the electronic wallet, as well as creates a Bitcoin address and private key. Multibit has Bitcoin wallets for different operating systems, while Hive offers a Bitcoin wallet that is OSX-based. Armory is a secured Bitcoin wallet while Darkwallet focuses on the anonymity feature.

Mobile Wallet

A mobile Bitcoin wallet comes in handy when a user wants to pay for goods and services from their smartphone. Compared to the desktop wallet, this type of Bitcoin wallet doesn't need the whole blockchain to work. It makes use of a simplified payment verification. Blockchain and Mycelium offer a Bitcoin wallet for Android phones. Kipochi uses the mobile phone number as the Bitcoin address.

Online Wallet

A Bitcoin wallet can be web-based. This means the private key is stored online. With an online wallet, a user can access their bitcoins anytime and anywhere. All a person needs is a computer device and an Internet connection. However, the user has no control over the private key. This means that he/she may lose their bitcoins if the online wallet is hacked.

To keep the Bitcoin wallet safe, it is necessary to protect the private key at all costs. It is possible to encrypt a Bitcoin wallet and have a difficult password to unlock it. However, it is still possible for hackers to access the wallet if the computer is infected by a malware, which records keystrokes. It is important to backup a Bitcoin wallet so that the user still has a copy of it if the computer crashes. Lastly, it is best to store the wallet offline. Cold storage keeps the private key offline. Some Bitcoin addresses can be stored in a hot wallet for easy spending. The bulk of the Bitcoin holdings are saved offline so that even if the computer is compromised, the bitcoins aren't lost.

Chapter 7:

How To Sell Bitcoin

Unlike buying bitcoins, selling the digital currency isn't extremely easy. Anyone who wants to sell bitcoins must first decide the method by which he/she wants to sell them. They can either sell the bitcoins online or sell them face-to-face.

In selling online, the individual can sell directly to another individual or through an exchange. If the person decides on direct trade, he/she can go to LocalBitcoins or Coinbase if they are in the United States of America. If they are in the United Kingdom, they can check out Bittylicious or BitBargain. These websites require sellers to register and the person can post an ad after registration. The site will usually alert the seller if there's an interested buyer. Negotiation are only between the two parties. However, trade completion is usually done on the website.

If selling is done through an online exchange, the seller is required to register on the exchange's website. A sell order is placed, indicating the volume and price per unit. When someone buys the bitcoins, it will be the exchange which will complete the transaction. Payment will be credited to the seller's account. The problem with this method is that the exchange may have issues with the banks or it may have liquidity problems. It is also possible to sell bitcoins for another crypto-currency. The seller has to pay a trade fee to the exchange.

Money can be withdrawn from an exchange through international wire transfers. If in Europe, money can be transferred to the bank account through the Single European Payments Area. These transfers often take days to be completed. An individual also has to pay expensive transaction fees. Banks may not allow customers to open an account if funds will come from Bitcoin trading. However, there are payment processors which allow such transactions.

Bitcoin buyers are often not required to go through an identification process. However, for sellers, they are required to show proof of identity. Thus, it is best for a Bitcoin seller to complete the verification process when he/she joins the exchange.

In selling bitcoins through face-to-face interaction, the seller will just scan the buyer's QR code to effect the transfer. They then accept the fiat money from the buyer. For in-person selling, both parties must agree on a price before the selling can commence. Most users base the price off a popular exchange. There are sellers who add a premium to the price for the buyer to pay for the convenience as well as incidental costs. When selling in-person, the seller should have somebody with them, especially if he/she will be carrying a lot of cash. The seller can use LocalBitcoins to look for possible buyers. The site has a rating scheme where both the buyer and seller can rate each other.

Chapter 8:

Difficulties Involving Bitcoin

Online Theft Of Bitcoins

It is possible to lose bitcoins to online thieves and there will only be more people trying to get involved in this crime as Bitcoin increases in popularity. However, the good news is that you can protect yourself. Needless to say, a person must ensure that they take the necessary measures to keep their Bitcoins safe and secure. There are lawless criminals who are able to hack third-party providers of Bitcoin wallets. Actually, even the personal computer isn't safe to these hackers. Most experts suggest that bitcoins should be kept in thumb drives which are not connected to personal computers when not in use.

There are also people who keep their private key written on paper and kept in their physical wallet. Other people have their private key engraved on a coin or ring. However, great care must also be exercised so that the coin, ring, or wallet is not accidentally lost.

Bitcoin Acceptance In The United States

Bitcoin as a currency is gaining ground around the world. It has become a low-cost way of transferring money, which poses a threat to companies like Western Union, PayPal, and even to credit card companies. Bitcoin transfers from one person to another are free of charge. However, Bitcoin transfers don't occur in real time because Bitcoin miners process transactions in around 10-minute batches. However, there are Bitcoin payment processors which can process transactions even quicker.

In the United States, the public has been warned against Bitcoin, although regulators haven't really made progress in deciding how the digital currency should be treated. There are certain countries which have started recognizing the new digital currency. However, the federal government is proceeding with extreme caution.

The bank accounts of Mt. Gox, the largest exchange for Bitcoin, have been closed in the United States because the company wasn't registered as a money transmitter. Afterwards, Bitcoin companies in the U.S.A. have also reported that banks no longer want to do business with them. However, the federal government has taken steps to understand Bitcoin so the general public will just have to wait in order to get more information on that.

Chapter 9:

The Legalities of Bitcoin

Of special interest groups to financial regulators, tax agencies, and law enforcement agencies, Bitcoin is taking center stage, especially now that more and more merchants are accepting it as a mode of payment. A lot of law enforcers and regulators are attempting to somewhat control it. Because the digital currency is only in its infancy, it is expected that a lot of people, legal authorities included, are trying their best to understand the concept of crypto-currency and their future.

The issue of Bitcoin legality is dependent on how it is used. Governments are very much concerned about it being used for money laundering activities because of its anonymity features. Also, these authorities are very much concerned that Bitcoin is decentralized and isn't controlled by a central authority.

In March 2013, the Financial Crime Enforcement Network in the United States of America released some guidelines about digital currencies. According to the guidelines, users of digital currencies can be considered as running a money services business. As such, they are to enforce measures under the Know Your Client and Anti-Money Laundering guidelines. On the other hand, the Commodity Futures Trading Commission of the United States of America has announced that it will regulate virtual currencies used as financial derivatives.

The Securities and Exchange Commission in the United States also hasn't issued any regulation on these crypto-currencies. However, an alert has been issued by the Office of Investor Education and Advocacy about Bitcoin being used in fraudulent investment plans. The U.S. Senate started looking into risks and threats of virtual currencies in August of 2013. According to the Department of Homeland Security, transactions using crypto-currencies don't have paper trails, so law enforcers and regulators are having a hard time following cases of illicit activities.

In the United States, every state has its own laws and regulators. In New York and California, both states are aggressively pursuing organizations involved with Bitcoin trading. Other states like Montana, South Carolina, and New Mexico don't have laws pertaining to money transfers. The state financial regulator in California wrote the Bitcoin Foundation in May of 2013, warning it of sanctions if it has proven that the foundation, in fact, is a money transmitting organization. In New York, the Department of Financial Services subpoenaed about 22 companies involved with Bitcoin activities in August of 2013. The department invited the Bitcoin companies in for a dialogue.

Needless to say, multiple banks have closed accounts of people involved with Bitcoin exchange operations. In November of 2013, the U.S. Senate scheduled hearings on federal and banking regulation issues. According to the Financial Crimes Enforcement Network, individuals who use Bitcoins to pay for goods and services aren't breaking any law. But, if the user acts as a money transmitter, he/she may be subject to regulation. Also, individuals who mine Bitcoins and exchange them for fiat currency aren't safe from regulation because they are acting as money transmitters. The Financial Crimes Enforcement Network considers Bitcoin exchanges as money transmitters and are, therefore, subject to regulation.

The Internal Revenue Service of the United States of America had ruled on the use of digital currencies in 2009. According to the IRS, individuals receiving income through a virtual economy are required to include it as taxable income. The ruling was based on guidance connected to hobby, business, gambling, and bartering income. The IRS also made the same ruling on digital currencies being used in real economies. Furthermore, it said the government agency is currently working with other agencies with regards to possible risks on tax compliance by electronic payment schemes which have remained   anonymous.

Conclusion

I hope this short book was able to help you learn more about the basics of Bitcoin, the different options you have, and how the future looks for this new currency. Now that you have learned the important factors surrounding Bitcoin, you can finally decide if you want to take the plunge, or if you can recommend it to your family and friends.

Plus, a little addition to your knowledge doesn't hurt, right? It's good to know about new innovations because it keeps you in the know and up-to-date in a world where every big city has groups dedicated to learning more about crypto-currencies.

Finally, if you learned anything from this book, please take the time to share your thoughts by sending me a message or even posting a review to Amazon.

Thank you and good luck in your journey!